WHAT TO DO AFTER & DURING ANY TYPE OF CARD READING
(Oracle, Angel, Lesson)

Steps that have never been taught until now!
"CARD THREADING WITH LOVE"

STARLET PARADIS

Balboa Press books may be ordered through booksellers or by contacting:

Balboa Press
A Division of Hay House
1663 Liberty Drive
Bloomington, IN 47403
www.balboapress.com
1 (877) 407-4847

ISBN: 978-1-9822-3446-1 (sc)
ISBN: 978-1-9822-3445-4 (e)

Library of Congress Control Number: 2019913455

Print information available on the last page.

Balboa Press rev. date: 10/22/2019

BALBOA.
PRESS
A DIVISION OF HAY HOUSE

FOREWORD

I've being doing readings for many years, for both myself and others, and always loved using cards for a self-development tool. I could ask the questions and get resonating answers, but I often wondered what to do with it all and so did people who were coming to me for a reading. Sometimes the answer was obvious, but I could not see how to apply it in my life and life of others to bring some tangible changes and results into reality. It almost felt like it kept us all waiting till things just show up. The question HOW do I do it? almost always remained unanswered.

It wasn't until I met Starlet who introduced me to her new way of Card Reading/Threading as she called it, that I really started to realize the impact a reading can actually have. I slowly started to see an answer to that question on "How to".

It opened up a whole new world of possibilities! Now, instead of reoccurring questions that kept on coming I started to see answers and actual steps that were bringing me into a place of manifesting in reality. Manifesting like you have never seen before. With such ease, grace and joy.

We ended up following our divine guidance with this new concept because we realized we have something new and exciting for everyone. Both existing readers and those who are just starting to learn about it. I am so excited to be a part of this as we teach this new way to all who choose it.

After seeing so many astonishing results while we did Card Threading for others we knew we have to write it as a book and offer it as a more in depth course, sharing this amazing new way and process with as many wonderful souls who are ready to manifest with Love, enjoying the entire process.

This definitely brings Card reading to a whole new level and I know you will enjoy it as much as I do.

With love,
Mayaa Dove

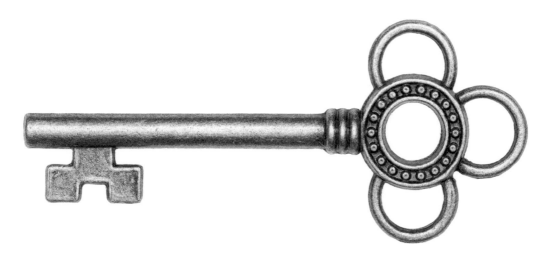

"The key to evolution is being open to the new, with respect to the old and bringing forth the techniques of new dimensional, and ways aligning us to our true essence."

Starlet Paradis

Have you ever felt your card reading, although pleasant, informational or inspiring, somehow left you feeling.............?

And you maybe thought:

"I know, this is awesome but what do I do?"

"Am I to.....................?"

Or "...........................?"

'Am I to.....................?"

It even may have left you speechless like it did for me and so many others that spoke to us about their own experience of other types of card readings, especially after having the experience of this New Way using any type of cards, bringing card reading to a whole new level.

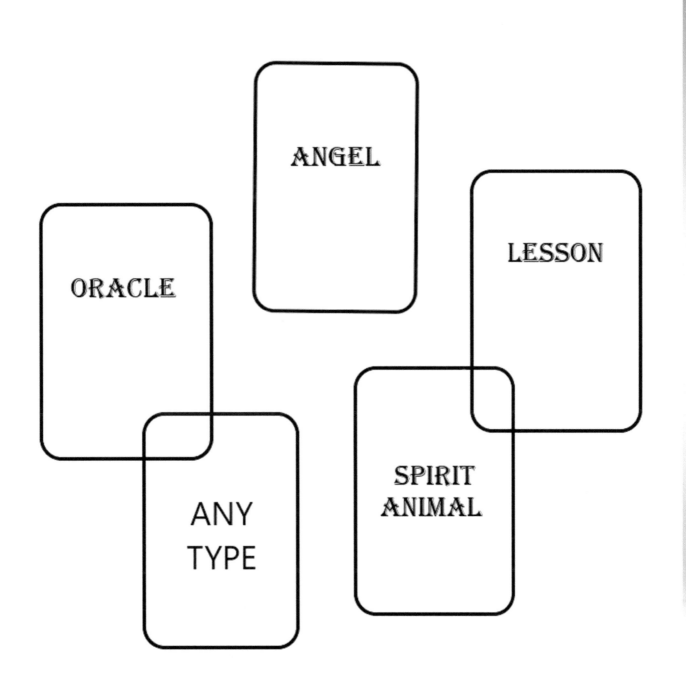

As a Reader/Card Reader or really anybody, you know you are the channel for what is going on during a reading. Then the person your reading for and sometimes even the reader can get as surprised as the person your reading for when responding to intuitiveness and what's going on. This is where the great "A-Ha" readings come from and the magic begins to happen.

What if I told you that I am an intuitive energy worker that has been presented with a new process that would take everything to the new level in record time? I have.

Mother God, the Council of Light and with the help of my friend Mayaa Dove, and myself Starlet Paradis welcome you to a new, innovative way of manifesting with cards with a way never been taught before. The reading is pretty general with clearing for a completion for a momentum and having an energetic plan in action, and having it manifest into form or in your reality through Love with Love.

I see the beauty in card reading and how easy it is to create or manifest through them. Without these steps that we will go through in the book or in our online course, I felt the reading although significant were incomplete so here is what we do to complete the process, bringing it all together and allowing the energetic process so the magic can begin.

Now with Divine Guidance I have been inspired to teach additional steps to the card readings to help bring it all together and help them manifest their story, with Love.

This may be for you personally if you like to do cards for yourself or for the card readers out there that are reading for clients. To explain a bit - when the cards are read, we pause, take in the information, we wonder or may get excited as the reading has been channelled by the person that is doing the reading, from a divine source but then what? We have told the client the story read it to them, help them see it through your eyes and brought it to life in the cards, but then what? There is some suggestions on what to do etc, but then what? That kept coming up for me and then through the eyes of my God Self, I seen how Card Treading works this made complete sense to me. Since the higher selves provide information that we so need to hear and heal, we can channel the appropriate steps for manifesting the changes, needed to move forward and make changes thru the reading. The client is already experiencing the emotions, and with emotion as fuel we can create the desired outcome. We will teach you the steps to create the outcome. The Follow through.

We manifest, thru a need, a desire, a temptation, choices.

While we read the cards,

The Love self guides

We create with the best outcome.

With Card Threading, we are in a space of a love vibration.

We create with Love and a Feeling Energy.

Whether it's thru sickness or in health we create, and we create with Love and the readiness of it.

We welcome you to this new way called Threading and will teach you to card read/thread with Love.

CARD READING, THREADING IS THE ONLY WAY WE DO CARD READINGS NOW. ANY TYPE OF CARDS (ORACLE, ANGEL, LESSON) CAN BE USED. CLIENTS ARE SO IMPRESSED SAYING HOW TRANSFORMING THE EXPERIENCE IS, A WHOLE NEW EXPERIENCE, NEVER EVER BEFORE, LOVING IT.

This Instructional BOOK, will help you Read Cards using the cards you already have (Oracle, Angel, Archangel, Lesson), a more in depth course is available online through The School Of Light.org

Card Threading with Oracle, Angel, Archangel, Lesson Cards are all work in what we do. Our platform is quite different but does work with these other cards and do not require there own special card deck. Understanding we use energy for manifesting, we assist and help through these steps necessary to complete the readings with the threading, manifesting change, with Love.

CHAPTERS

CHAPTER 1

INTRODUCTION

Hello, We are very excited for you to join us on this new innovative way of reading cards, any type of cards and creating the momentum, and the change to manifest.

I suggest that before you start anything day, your day a reading or for yourself, you Center and Align. This is a centering to You, your true connection to your authenticity, to your true you, You Are.

Once you have established the centering you will find your thoughts get centered to you effortlessly, if you are an empath and feel others you will feel much better much more collected, more in the present. This daily practice has been very beneficial for me and for many others, children included.

Center & Aligning course is available online at www.theschooloflight.org or at different events.

The second part of this is about getting you ready, being ready. When you center and align yourself you still may feel prompted by your high self to shield when you are going into a different places/situation, clients, even if you have known these people or places all your life. There maybe something you are not knowing but your high self, your guides are warning you about.

Shielding is important if you really feel the need, it is for your highest good to advise or guide you to the approach that best works and suits you and how you see it.

I do want to explain here that in the intelligence of source when you shield there is a prediction that is realized. When one comes in with fear it is really superficial, and it will not be beneficial for you to shield, almost may make it worse in some cases you will attract what it is you feel strongest about. If you are fearing, you will attract things to fear. Coming from a place of Love is where you will want to be. We have not used a shield for years as we are ascending, things have changed and rather quickly at times even through out a single day. And we are prompted to be in an energy of love and all the energy of it. To attract love, we must be coming from love, to be love, able to enjoy the experience of love, attracting what gives you more of what love is to you.

In my practice, I surround myself with love and sometimes different light, follow your guidance. We as a divine being follow our guidance, what ever feels right for you is what you need to do. In different times for different reasons I have used what looks like a Energetic blanket at different times when I am guided. As an example, putting on a coat to stay warm, not putting a coat on to keep out the cold, placing a intention to be warm or placing a intention to fight the cold. Which one is easier? The interesting thing about energy it attracts what it is, not what it isn't.

If you can be in a state of love, seeking in kindness, with generosity, with love, you are coming from a love way of thinking, feeling ,creating.

Surrounding yourself with Love you will see, feel the energy of it swaying , twirling, swirling around you. Complete Love as you grounding to Love.

I find there are less energy entanglements, unnecessary entanglements that may come from other energies.

CHAPTER 2

PREPARING FOR THE READING

Surrounding yourself with Love, and grounding to Love brings the reading into perfect alignment for both you and the person you're doing the threading with.

When your feeling you're centered, surrounded with Love, calling in the Pillars of light is your next step. You may feel/know or maybe see them as they stand around, your room and you may be recognizing them in various shades of color.

As the Council has initiated the translucent energy of time where all matter appears as it will in various pigments, the energy of these lights will be that of authority. All you need to do is be present within these columns of light as the energies of the great force of Love shall secrete through all and bring forth all that is good.

Colors are apparent for the Purpose of the Pillars, when this is apparent whether you know it or not, the outside forces should not interfere with you unless for some reason have been called in by speaking about something over and over again, or for a extremely good reason. You will feel the difference easily, push them back away from the space as you clear whatever the entanglement may have been about, clearing very easily with the light energy, the energy the pillars radiate within them. This energy is very strong, very light.

Being that all energy has its own radiation it will depict a sense off peace, tranquility, calmness having a positive experience, effect for the person your reading for.

The energy will depict energy that will be perfect for the session for the reader, the recipient for all.

Planetarian Energy, Earth Energy, Animal Energy, all energy as every energy has a purpose, and may show up in your reading. Trusting that it is best and for a reason for whoever you're reading for.

Whatever comes up for them for this reading, you will easily recognize, feel or know it in the way you usually do, intuitively reading from Love for this specific type of reading, while enhancing the energy in the energetic Pyramid. The Pyramid of light energy enhances vibration enough to partake in the energy work that's being done, for them, with them, with the greatest intention.

CHAPTER 3

GIVING A HAND UP

Now that the person has come for a read, stay worry free as you are the channel, staying grounded to love, in case you missed that earlier, allow the magic of your high self do the rest. Trust messages that come through while you and begin. Allow the person that is there for the reading to relax as everything falls into place. Now as you are being taken cared of, go on with whatever is. Channel relax and be attentive.

This is where you light a candle, helps everyone relax and brings more light into the session. Generally, we light a tea light up for that session only as every session is unique and we take a fresh tea light every time, helps keep it clear. At the beginning of each session we start the session and light it while the person is present. When the session is over the candle is to be blown out while you and the client/recipient are together, wrap the candle or place it in their "to go box". When they arrive at where ever they are going they can do whatever they want with it. They may want to light it again and finish it up or who knows, the important thing is that they take it with them. this will help them release, let go, and the healing continues and so does the intention for the manifestation. This will help them release, and the intention for their story released and their story can continue for them, the detanglement is quick and easy, and done.

If the person your doing the reading for has no visual concept of what's going on, it's okay, not everybody does. If they get running after, talking a lot about whatever let them talk, feeling relaxed about the process and if they are worried about things bring them back – energetically take them by their hand and bring to that energetic pyramid place and relax literally sit back relax.

This can happens when the person your doing the reading for doesn't know what to expect or fears the answer or has been through lots of turmoil, an illness, fears, lacks confidence in themselves so they keep going back to the same/known place that seems to be the norm as they have never had an experience of such high vibration in this new way of reading it maybe an unknown feeling to them. They will try to hide or switch off, as sometimes their Ego may be dictating fear, or testing you, or not really knowing what they want. It's your job to keep them in a space of Love. Keep bringing them back to a good feeling place. The place where it feels like they are wanting to be but may be tempted to go back down to the energy they have been living, talking about, worried about, been feeling more of for so long they have become addicted and maybe stuck in old ways. Even though they want new, they keep going back to the old and your job is to bring them to their new higher vibration where change can take place and manifesting begins. The opportunity of real change to happen even quicker.

Important to mention here that alignment is always Perfect, Mother God wouldn't want to see it any other way.

In some you may notice that there is an introduction time as client's Divinely guided guides may enter, as there is a clearing that is best suited before you even begin. This will all come. Follow your high self, your intuitiveness, your messages, and trust. This type of session (séance) is all about Love and having the reading in the vibration of it. When you have a person come in and they get so relaxed and feel a higher vibration they will have a tendency of attracting more Love, good fun, joy, kindness, happiness and that is what we all would love to see as healers, readers, energy intuitives, everyone for everyone.

CHAPTER 4

WORKING WITH THE HIGHER SELF

Calling upon their High Self – will clear out any shadows or misguided guides. As you likely already know they may try to interfere or influence the reading.

In case you keep on feeling/seeing shadows that you feel need to be removed you can call for assistant, like a spirit animal (dog, cat, dragon, water buffalo, etc.) angel, archangel or whatever comes to mind and introduce your guide to assist in whatever way is best suited. They are divine helpers that gather up the energy for transmutation or to give it to God, to do whatever is best for that particular session. Free of judgment to what may come up and flow with it, seeing the truth, taking your time as time spent with you is precious.

What people may not realize is that, when we are gifted (I feel we all are), what I have seen to be is that we tend to hang onto guides and shadows to understand the light and what we carry. What we sometimes don't realize is that our guides, angel guardians are assisting us for different time periods of our life, and we need shadows to determine different factors in our life. When you are finally getting a lot of clearing happening you will feel happier, feel safe with a few and not hang on to them all. As they need to release and move on to the next timeline, next person, etc. As you know that the god within you, has your highest good as always in all that you do.

During healing, all who is best suited will be called upon for this reading/threading. Go with the flow and allow everything and anything that comes up.

Be in the moment, present and you will be aware of any feelings in your physical or emotional body that come up and be ready to accept and read it for what it truly is.

This Card Reading is in its Divinity and will less likely bring in false hope, lies or confusing information.

Reactions to this method are quite stimulating, how to receive energy of the change, the new story and let go of the old.

It will teach you techniques to remove barriers that you may have learned or took on from others or are carrying from past lives or are not necessary as your truth is your truth.

You might have developed a technique that has helped you in different style of readings and may no longer work quite like that for this style as the connection to Love in this new technique is adding the new to this way of healing with change, manifesting throughout the reading. This will keep you fit enough to always be perfectly aligned for every now and grounded to Love. Example or metaphor Aligning yourself with your truest form of you is like a pencil, you need to stay sharpened.

It's a new way of being, we seem to be manifesting quicker than ever before.

CHAPTER 5

THE "KEY"

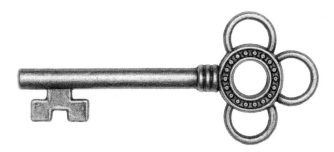

The Key to evolution is being open to the new, with respect to the old and bringing forth the techniques of new dimensional, and ways aligning us to our true essence.

We are transmuting energies that no longer serve us anyway so why not stay aligned to evolving as we are such evolved being from the inside. We have powers and energy we haven't even tapped into yet, for some reason we hang on to the familiar and stay indifferent, when different is the new norm.

If you can stay open to the new you will be at your Home, your You, You Are The Key, the answers reside within you.

CHAPTER 6

OPENING UP YOUR CHANNEL

Next step to the Card Threading is being available and open to receiving the messages that you're about to experience with every action. As every action card is being read and is being activated into action.

Our Intention is to see Divine truth, always with Love, grounded to Love.

You may be experiencing the energies that might be of another dimension. They are there to guide you into action. Why the itchy nose? Eyes tearing? Goosebumps? Twitching? A poking?

This is the time to ask for purpose of their reading as you are choosing the deck of cards or shuffling through the cards from deck(s) you were guided to choose from and trust the answer that comes. Choose card decks that feel right for each particular session.

For example, a client comes with expression of wanting to know what to do next in life, for business, or what their purpose is or should they stay married, and so on… Trust that right decks/cards have been presented/shown to you using the cards you already have. Now as the story unfolds the true answers unfold and much more. Remember that the High Self may be explaining much different than the human client is thinking or worried about. An example would be something like this: the recipient is asking information about a contest that he or she is wanting to win and wanting to go to Jamaica to compete for it and maybe a way to get there. When clearly the Higher Self can show a more direct approach for the desired outcome, perhaps the contest the person will win is in California so the reading can be directing them to go to California first.

On your part, all fears and doubts are to be removed for any session. Ask for it before you even start- "Clearing from all fears and doubts for this reading for this session."

You're real, this is real, you're here doing it, you're here, you're getting answers. There's not doubt anymore. It's real. You're real. You're a celebrity and you're playing your part in the game of life.

You are Charismatic, Imaginative, Luminous, Confident Being, Authentic, Inspiring, Passionate, Magnetic, Public, Independent, Noble, Generous, Unique.

Asking for the purpose of a reading will help you to choose the deck or decks you will be using. Card threading can be used with all types of cards, but the key is to keep open to whatever feels "right", or whatever you feel inclined to say or do as you are channeling the energies for this type of reading. Reads like channeling the energies for this type of reading.

When it comes to how many draws and how to place the cards, you will simply know. Whatever feels right is right. It may be 3, 5, 8 cards or more. It can be circle, cross, heart shape whatever comes up – the sequence is not important as much as how the story will explain itself. Be open to whatever the placement shows up or how many cards you draw, as there will be a reason for what you are doing, follow what intuitively feels right for you.

The cards may jump out of the deck for you or you may feel the ones that come, if you feel they may not be a part of the reading its okay to move it around or even remove them and replace them as you unfolding the story the card may have changed and been replaced by another. Once you start placing the cards in sequence you will see, and all will make perfect sense.

In our kind of reading/threading, cards usually like to unfold left to right for the client, right to left for you. Read left to right for the person who you are reading for.

Relax as you reveal perfectly the story for your client.

The recipient will appreciate your dedication and time you are spending with them. Time is energy, by giving it time you have plenty of it.

As you read the cards the perfect picture and message appear. Now that you have gone over the cards one at the time their story reveals itself and questions are being answered. For this way of reading we are reading the cards from love perspective and involving the person you are doing the reading for, having them participate in their story energetically.

In this example: We have a card that shows the name of the card, the picture and explanation of the card. Depending on what the story is telling you decide to explain it as it's already happening. The energy will be enhanced so answers come in the most loving way. Unfolding the message in a way that is threading into action. For example there is a trail, it runs through the forest and has a branch laying over, obstructing the path and now with your intuitiveness you will see them jumping over the branch or lifting, moving it out of the way clearing their path. The path now being free and clear to pass. Here you may even show the client or recipient how everything is being cleared or even having them clear it with their minds eye seeing it happen.

You can do this as the cards reveal themselves but most certainly before you or they choose a trump card which will finish up the story.

Always keeping the client engaged. Leading you to the solution, the next answer, the next question which maybe in the next card. The next Threading will be the next card and then the next and so on… creating a momentum that will surely manifest into form. After the story has been unfolded ask if there's any questions to be answered and follow your guidance, your channel. As you're done with hearing the questions and have red the cards now is the time to choose one Connector card.

CHAPTER 7

IT'S REALLY HAPPENING

A "Connector Card"

You might be feeling to ask the client or recipient to pick a deck in which to draw a card from. It may feel right even to ask the recipient to pick the connector as well. In any case go with the feeling, your intuitiveness, your knowing. Once you have done a few readings you will know and it will come very easy, very easy.

The connector card is the card that will reveal the next course of action. It may reveal a question that needs answering. This may even bring up a question for the recipient which may have created the discomfort needed to thread the energy from one to another. Discomfort may be unanswered question, hidden answer that reader hasn't heard or answered before, but the energy is needed to be cleared to create the positive momentum to bring in the new.

If you feel a card is not coming, you may need to revisit the cards and have the higher self show you what you missed in the first pass. You may feel that you were not clear in the response to an answer so it is coming up for a reason and that is okay as the recipient may have been declaring what I call war on themselves and smudged the picture, the answer. Its all okay. You got it now. Clearing the energy.

If you feel clear and ready you can choose The Connector card which gets everything in motion.

Has the client responded to the change? Feel the difference in the energy.

Is there a solution?

Are they ready?

And if so, it is.

The client or you or maybe both of you may feel the shifting going on as you release any blocks or any contraband which may have been creating blocks or disguises from the truth, putting everything in to prospective. If ever there was a time that you are to be clear it is now. Relax and allow the truth to be told. Take your time feel love, feel excited, ask the person your reading for to relax, its a huge experience for them. life changing.

As the story is already in motion and client feels confident about change that is going to take place, the story that is unfolded, choose the Trump Card.

Asking the recipient to take part in any part of the reading, asking what they see or feel what the card is showing them will only solidify the manifestation. If you are getting the divine guidance to have them point something out pick a card or read a card, etc then follow your guidance, whatever feels right.

Remember vibration is key, keeping it very clear for them to see, feel the energy shift, the change that will occur. In any case go with your feeling/your intuitiveness/your knowingness, once you have done a few you will know and Love this new way of reading.

This type of card reading is open, and you may see the cards differently each time you look at the same card as it is different for different people. If they're upside down, it shows that client needs to look at it and point out what they notice the most, let them read it themselves, tell you how they see it.

Don't focus on general meaning of the card but instead take notice of what stands out and use it as a tool. Example - there's writing that's red but you're only noticing the yellow then the color is guiding you to follow the yellow. It's like a timekeeper who is telling you this is the time to take action. To notice patterns, details that are part of creation. Always remember to keep it light.

Everyone truly knows what they shouldn't do they are usually looking to know what to do or a answer to their questions and if there is any action required.

Love, laugh… They been taught thru time to laugh only when this happens and cry when this happens. You are showing them a different way. Manifesting through the card reading.

As you shuffle the cards when client is present, they are setting the intention for the reading with their Higher Self.

The next step for the Connector card is, as you are shuffling the cards their higher self is bringing forth the best card or picture that will tie it all in, your intention is to be clear as the higher selves communicate with each other and present the connector first, then the trump.

If for some reason you are stalling or feeling hesitant you may need to clarify something up just a bit more, maybe even going through the cards again, maybe there is a bit more to their story that need to unravel or unravelled after you read it, revealing more to you now.

Once you pick the connector card, place it in front of all others, front for the client, see how it connects thru to all the story that turned up with the reading. As the story that unfolded itself in that card goes thru them all, it shifts the energy to allow the reality to mirror, the energy shifts for the physical manifestation. Making sure that it all makes sense to the story that the recipient is manifesting, lining up and answers the unanswered questions the person may still have. Here you may even go over the story recapping, going over the change (example: clearing the path, removing debris, floating in a cloud, looking at her mate, etc.)

The next step is to place the cards one on top of each other, in a pile (no matter how many) with the connector card last, you will feel which cards go where in your pile, they merge? Once they merge you will pick a Trump card that will seal the deal. Sometimes you will feel that Connector card already worked as a Trump card. You will also sometimes feel to engage the client to pick the Connector or the Trump card or both as it gives them sense of creating their reality. It gives them opportunity to participate in their own life, follow your intuition. Having them participate is more fun for them and you.

Also, it is sometimes needed to have it locked into their psyche, making it more concrete, any kind of action helps them step into change, so there is only moving forward into what they want. It is done now. The shift will be as it becomes, in their vibration it is, in their illusion it must appear.

CHAPTER 8

THE TRUMP CARD

Tips, Reminders and "The Trump"

Keep your area as clear as possible.

Ground to Love

Have your thoughts in check, remember your reading is coming from Love, meaning it will be different than you are maybe used to. You will be clearing as you are reading their story. You are also helping to Create momentum for change. Good change for them with you, through you, so be positive, excited for them. As an example if a part of the story, a card maybe is showing you an energy where an elephant walks on to a platform representing strength and they will need to see themselves as one, seeing the strength within them, so reveal it to them with guidance and determination that they are the elephant energy. They are the strength, the inspiration without doing anything, use the cards, the story as a tool. Another example, if cards showing someone walking on a path, fence or wall, help them by walking them to the end of path, push the fence over, see them on the other side free. Help them see, feel see the vision that is coming to you for them.

If a card shows a book for example, see it as already written. Bring its reality into focus. And allow the recipient or client to participate if there is an opportunity. It's for you to engage the client into the process of this amazing tool of clearing, healing and creating the next best step, bringing it into their reality as the present experience, revealing itself to them for real.

The Card Threading is very exciting tool, as a director/reader, you will help them merge with the new energy by placing their hand over the card, the final card, trump card is on top of the pile, their story have been threaded and cards placed in the pile. This is the final step. Merging with the energy, vibrating within the new.

As they merge, IT IS.

It's like taking timeline and threading into Now, into the manifested. Before you move the elements in the story, the card it stays as future or suggestion or idea, but after threading it is here and now and done.

A more in depth course can be taken online or in person where you will receive the Certificate of Authenticity automatically inspiring you to manifest with Cards, called Card Threading. This magnificent tool that we are teaching and can help you manifest whatever it is you are ascending towards. There are many magnificent card decks that have been inspired and created by many great artists that are usable for this, our type of reading. Card Reading/Threading, with this different platform will compliment whatever you are already doing for yourself and for others. You will inspire yourself to attend the healing and prepare you for your creation to be realized by you or by whoever you read and threaded for. We have magnificent results with this technique taking you out of the way with the receiving wide open clearing manifesting tool.

This technique is transforming in ways that cannot be easily described in writing but in personal experience and having fun with this way of reading. We invite you to have your own experience of manifesting with cards, Card Threading at its best by taking a more in-depth course online through the School of Light.org

www.theschooloflight.org

You will feel the amazing transformation right in front of your eyes!

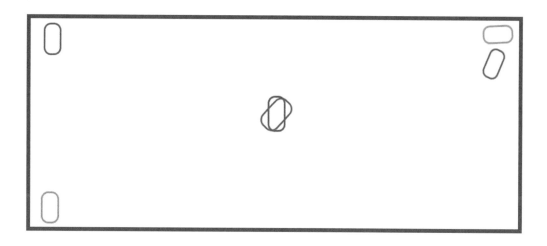

Thank You!

~ Acknowledgment to ~

All Beings who helped and participated with it all.
Archangels, Angels, Ascended Masters, All Masters, My High Self, Time and All,

Thank You.

Mayaa Dove

Thank you for being there, working with me, inspiring me to offer these intuitive teachings to others. I look forward to this journey as we continue to offer these new inspiring ways, and our insight to others.

Creator & Award Winning Author of "Your Sacred Wealth Code" Unlock Your Soul Blueprint For Purpose & Prosperity www.Soulutionary.com

Prema Lee Gurreri

Starlet goes outside the box with her willingness and openness to explore and intuitively develop innovative ways, resulting in showing her ways to heal and manifest with love, where rules, names or labels are not needed anymore - only truth. This is where one can feel confident, powerful, inspired, fulfilled, loved in and out, judgment free. She welcomes you to a new era where all is possible, infinite possibilities manifesting from a place of Love.

She marvels at the idea that people are coming more into alignment with themselves and is particularly in awe of innovative ways in which they can get there. It brings her happiness to know that more and more people are truly falling in love with themselves.

As a facilitator, working with the light, following her Divine calling, she has come across many abilities that will help those wishing to help themselves, be in their own love, be with others, and radiating their highest form of being.

She believes in helping others in ways that they can accelerate themselves to that place of being if that's what they choose.

She works with Love, Energy, Councils of Light and has spent countless hours experiencing, teaching, observing and has learned new ways that have been intuitively introduced to her. At some point a card reader, reader, reiki master, energy intuitive, healer and much more but felt it's time to present teaching ways of what she feels and knows it to be.

As a facilitator, visionary, spokesperson and channeler, she loves what she does.

Her work speaks for itself, more than any words or recommendations could describe. She invites you to enjoy for your own experience, seeing and feeling for yourself and Welcomes You to the New!

Printed in the United States
By Bookmasters